MANIFESTING

A Master's Manual

by

Khit Harding

Copyright 1988 by Khit Harding

ISBN 0-9615868-2-6
All rights reserved under International and Pan American Copyright
Conventions.

Published by Adams Publishing Company, P.O. Box 356, Eastsound,
Washington 98245.

Cover Art and Book Design by Bruce Adams

First printing 1988

The text of this book is based on the teachings of Ramtha the
Enlightened One as channelled by JZ Knight during the Novem-
ber, 1986, intensive The Power to Manifest. This book is designed to
provide pleasure and information on the subject of manifesting.
The author, publisher and JZ Knight shall have neither liability nor
responsibility to any person with respect to any loss or damage
caused or alleged to be caused directly or indirectly by the information contained in this book.

This is the second volume in the Becoming Series. The first volume is
entitled BECOMING, A MASTER'S MANUAL. If you wish to be on our
mailing list, please send your name and address to Adams Publishing Company at the above address.

Thank you Father Within Me.

Thank you JZ . I love you for opening the door to light.

Thank you Bruce and Sasha. I love you for being you.

Thank you for the unconditional love and support of my dear friends.

Especially thank you Leslie Tomlin, Marcia Keizer Batey, Claude Golden, and Ernest Kanzler.

Thank you Mama and Daddy for always encouraging me, and thank you Deborah for loving what I did.

Thank you everyone who said "Yes" to life.

Thank you to each person who bought BECOMING, A MASTER'S MANUAL. You made MANIFESTING, A MASTER'S MANUAL possible.

What is this book for? Not only is it to bring forth the understanding of manifestation, it is also to bring forth that which is termed YOU, that you know who you are, that you get a picture of what you are on the inside, and that you get a very clear understanding of where you are in your awakening and where you are in your dream.

This book is dedicated to you.

"Behold God"

From the Lord God of My Being

Unto the Father Within,

Unto that which I AM,

Come forth this hour

Into knowingness,

Indeed, into wisdom.

So be it.

To life

Forever and ever and ever.

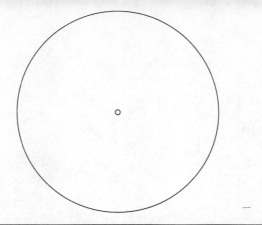

LEARNING TO MANIFEST IS YOUR DIVINE HERITAGE.

It is the jewel that makes life reality.

It is important for you to know that you have already started the process of manifestation just to be where you are now. This is the basis from which to learn more.

You are worth it.

What makes you unique and grand and beauteous is that you are divine in the greatest sense of that word. Divine.

You are precious.

You see the world as limited because you see yourself as limited.

You find many reasons why you are not so precious or grand, beauteous or unique, and if given the opportunity you can elaborate in great depth upon all that you are not, but that is your limited perception of yourself because your only mirrors are one another and you lack the absoluteness that you are wondrous things, that you are God.

What reflects back to you that you are God? Very little. You are hypnotized, you are entranced, you are convinced of your withoutness because everyone else is without. If the mirror doesn't reflect the power that emanates from vivid dancing eyes, if it doesn't show you your light, if your frontal lobe isn't visible enough to show you how powerful your reasoning is, then you can only assume your identity is what is in the mirror, your identity is what you see in everyone else around you. And after awhile, the image that is you becomes the image of limitation — you know that you are not divine, you are not grand, because that is what you perceive of yourself through the vision of others.

Your identity is only viewed through interactions with other people whose identity is perceived through you.

You are inclined to complain because the moment you get somewhere in your life, you go back and recount the misery that it took
to get there instead of laughing! That comes from not knowing
I AM. It comes from not realizing how powerful you are. You take
a step forward and you dance back twice! You have not learned
to hold to your forward step and revel in the sublimely precious
moment you have created.

What you hear or read or see or experience will be effective when
you take the step forward and revel in what you have gained
without looking back.

Learn to embrace this power.

See YOU. You are BEAUTIFUL. See your light dance around you.

Because of you there is grand hope for all the mirrors. It only takes
one to look into the magic mirror and see a great and profound,
unique truth, for the rest of the mirrors to begin to wake up.

Part of the hypnotic influence that you have encountered for eons, lifetime after lifetime after lifetime, is the inducement through political rhetoric and religious dogma that has separated you away from God the Father, the Grand Intelligence, the Great Cause, the Principle of Life.

Through separateness you have engaged in war, you have created disease, you have erected invisible walls and boundaries and there is a rampant amount of distrust in your world because you are not in the flow of the Supreme Intelligence. When you refuse to go into Knowingness, you step outside of it and you create friction.

Part of the image of the mirror defies your divinity. You cannot own that you are God because it goes against what is proper, correct and social, and after so many lifetimes away, it takes an arduous effort to come back to it.

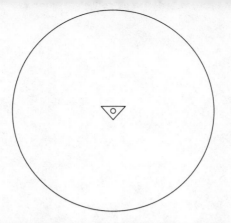

BEHOLD GOD

One of the greatest teachings of all, of all words issued forth into that which is termed most common speech, is

BEHOLD GOD.

If you know and embrace that, it is all you ever need. That know-ingness is everything.

How many bodies have you worn? Many. Like your closet with all your clothing and adornments. That is like another body.

What has been constant is the attitude, the personality self, and only when you have lived upon this plane, the son of God manifest in flesh and blood - Godman in this greatest dimension of God - only when you have lived through that, can you become a Christ. Godman. Man realizing the totality of his divinity, realizing that he is a mirror of God. Only this way.

A mirror tells you, through an assortment of runners, that prophecy is manifesting against many oppositions. The mirror tells you that you are God, that integral life is the cosmos of the atom, that the flare of the sun that is violent, giving birth to knowingness, is one and the same of the all that is the All.

You are the greatest mystery. The discovery of what you are behind those eyes, what you are and what your meaning and purpose are — that is the mystery.

In this hour you live in another body, another time, speculative though it is, and it is an adventure, it is a gift, but in the adventure and the gift, you do not know that you are God.

THE MAGIC OF MANIFESTATION IS SIMPLICITY. It is profoundly
simple. It is what you think you are that is doing the manifestation.

God is not an embittered god who passes judgement of good and
bad upon his creation. His creation is called Life, Nature, and it
flows into forever, continuously perfecting its beauty by every
adventure.

His creation has never been judged. It has been allowed.
YOU ARE GOD. However long it takes you to hear it, if it is 10,000
repetitions, listen, for there is nothing greater than the arisen Christ.
There is nothing more wonderful than a world perceived in harmony, rather than contention. YOU ARE GOD.

God, Supreme Life, is without judgement, is without positive/
negative, is profound knowingness, is called forever, and governs
all kingdoms under the manifestation of thought into mass.

Power of manifestation. It is sublimely simple, but without it life does
not exist, for the miracle of life is in the determination of the manifestation. To have control of your destiny is outrageous, and yet
that is the power that directs the manifestations.

You are known by your light, your energy that is the frequency that emanates from your mass, and the frequency that holds together the mass is the great Spirit of Your Being, the great God of Your Being, the Lord of Your Being. The Lord of Your Being is the composite of divinity.

The God of Your Being is your auric field, or your spirit. This entity is very visible.

This is the key that opens the door: ONLY THROUGH KNOWLEDGE ARE YOU GOING TO BE FREE ENOUGH TO EMBRACE THE TRUTH. And in that freedom you will be able to embrace this most divine heritage that has remained latent within you, but only when you get over the obstacle of not knowing that you are going to know.

It is only when you own the knowledge, it is only that moment when you allow yourself to embrace all of the possibilities, that you will own the power of direct manifestation. You won't get it any other way. If you do this you will touch the inner god, and what you desire to come forward to know will do so in a unified essence that is electrical and powerful and – so be it – you have learned to manifest your first desire, focused.

This is the strategy: let the divinity of what you are begin to bloom into all sorts of possibilities.

When all of the creation of this beloved planet, the emerald of this universe, was set in motion, when God breathed into the creations of the plants, the fishes and the animals, it was not that they were laid bare and created leaf by leaf.

The breath of life was an idealism manifested into cellular mass, born into aqueous substance like a womb.

When it is said the gods breathed life into the living planet, that god, which was thought, manifested into the creativity of light, took thought, conceived a thought in an unlimited manner, without judgement good or bad, and embraced it through the soul. Then that god formed the vision, and through the soul embracing the frequency of the thought that enamored the body, the soul recorded the feeling and the vision was formed in the seat of the mind, the imagination. It is through EMBRACING that the thought can be lowered by emotion into mass. The breath of life that was breathed into the cells was the ideal of the whole. The cell carries the pattern of the whole. That was the breath of life.

Every cell contains the power of manifestation through the embraced thought of the god who conceived it. Learn to embrace a thought.

Everything on earth is of thought, embraced by an intelligence, born of the mass of that intelligence into a frequency called three dimensional. This is the slow evolution of thought realized.

When all the thoughts created by the gods were set into the single cell, holding the frozen thought of "embrace" as a pattern to grow by, when this was all done, the gods desired to be OF mass. After all, how could a light embrace and smell the deep perfume of a rose? How could a light hold the velvetness in its hands? It couldn't. It was on a different frequency: the gods were gods of light.

Man was created as an experiment through the same "breath of life" experience as the rose was created, except that he would be the instrument, the vehicle, of great intelligence that could hold its creation, the rose, and smell its wondrous perfume.

The rose has evolved to become the completion of the god's dream. In the beginning, there wasn't "the rose"; there was the embraced manifestation of the rose. The god's breath of life, through life, has evolved to become the crystallization of the first cell.

Man was conceived in the same manner. He is HIS cell, and the breath of life blown into him evolved over eons to become what he is this day. And only through living could man the god evolve, like his rose. You have evolved to a kingdom that you created. You lived the adventure to see the rose.

What happened to the original manifesters of destiny, the gods of light who created the rose and the fishes of the sea, who put balance into the ecosystem? What happened to you?

You are caught in a dream you think is reality. You have gone to sleep and it is an uphill struggle to wake up.

Call back the order of your original creativity: YOU the forgotten gods. You ARE that spirit.

You were once a great god. The light around you is the remaining particle of your origin. The mass that you are in is the vehicle that allows you the adventure of life that you set into motion eons ago.

YOU ARE THE ORIGINAL MANIFESTATION OF YOUR OWN POWER.

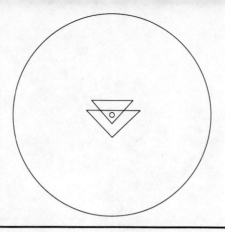

YOU CAME HERE TO LEARN HOW TO MANIFEST

You will never know and own that power until you know WHO you are, until you KNOW you are worth it. WORTH IT.

You have been taking a back seat to your own divinity.

You have given your power away. You have worshipped gods, gurus, kings, governments, warriors, conquerors and your next-door neighbor. You have allowed yourself to be intimidated into believing you are a no thing.

You went to sleep when you closed down your divinity and you shut off every divine knowingness. You have dreamed yourself into one-third brain power. The only consciousness your brain is open to receive is the lower frequency called "social consciousness," and that is called surviving.

Your brain is asleep. You are living a dream. You are so powerful that you have forgotten your original light. You have forgotten why you are here. You have become civilized in a mode of limited thinking . Latent Christ, latent consciousness, unconditional love are locked within your sleeping brain. You have closed down your brilliant knowingness. YOU ARE GOD.

Now, what does this have to do with manifestation? Everything. If you were powerful enough to shut down, you are powerful enough to wake up!

There is one thing to remember about knowing who you are:

TAKE CREDIT FOR EVERYTHING YOU HAVE DONE.

When you become outrageous, you become a genius.

When you step out of the circle of the mundane, you become the original.

If you knew how great you were, how powerful your words and your actions, you would be a living Christ this moment to the whole of the world.

You think that your body is all that you are. You are looking for the wrong thing in your identity. It is what is inside you and around you that is all that you are.

Live not for your body but live for your spirit which governs the body, then the body will be transfigured and illuminated.

You come into manifestation and begin to look at all the mirrors around you, whose only identity is a body. You begin to shut down clear knowingness when you come back to this life. You knew what this game was all about before you chose to return.

Your body has a destiny - it is destined to do certain things. You spend all of your life buffing and polishing and struggling, whatever your game is, DOING something with your body.

When it comes to manifestation, your body - supreme god and wonderful - often gets in the way, because the body lives in a different time flow than you do. Emotion packs powerful change into it, and that which awakened when it came back, went back to sleep because its whole identity was through the physical.

You are beautiful. There is nothing other than beauty in life.

Just that you ARE is a miracle.

This plane is the apex dimension, for this is clearly thought manifested into the fervor of three dimensional fact. This is the apex of the kingdom of God. Manifestation must pass from thought to light to lower electrum, from lower electrum into negative and positive electricity, lowered into a radical frequency to become gross matter where it formulates the cellular mass of the ideal. The ideal becomes the pattern of destiny through the cell.

Every cell has its own soul which holds together the memory of the cell. The soul keeps intact the chromosome structures of its parents. The parents create the chromosome genetic structure through coagulated emotion — their attitudes and how they lived created their genes.

You chose your parents based on their cellular mass and their genetic structures. When the body comes together, it is endowed not only with the genetic body, but with the possibility of disease because what creates the heritage of disease is attitude. If the attitude creates a sickness in the body, it also crystallizes in the chromosomes.

Everything you think in a powerful emotional attitude in this life manifests. If you find yourself in contention with others because they are a mirror and you don't like what you see about yourself, that attitude makes its way through thought, emotion, electricity, lower electrum and ends up in the body.

You manifest emotionally what you think of yourself.

What gave you the right to do with your life as you have done? Free will. It is an immutable law.

The moment you were born of thought into light, you became that law. It is irrevocable, because it is the premise of life. You have had full reign over your adventure.

There is not one thing in your life that you did not manifest. Somewhere you had a dream. Somewhere you embraced the escapades of another mirror. Somewhere you have run the gamut of fantasies from the most violent to the most sublime.

YOU SET UP YOUR TOMORROW WITH EVERY IMAGINATION, EVERY FANTASY, EVERY DAYDREAM, EVERYTHING YOU DO THAT CREATES EMOTION IN YOUR SOUL.

Now, the body lives in a different time flow. The body lives in the past. It doesn't move as swiftly as your mind moves. What you are experiencing this moment is not yet involving the body. Your body can be years behind what you are learning now.

Why are you confused in your life? Why are things happening to you now? Because if they are in the physical now, they are the manifestation of what you felt perhaps five years ago. Why are you still being haunted by what happened years ago? Why isn't it resolved? Because the body is now manifesting the past feeling. The soul in the cell is activating that pattern of attitude, and that attitude begins to become the blue corona around your body that is continually feeding your consciousness.

When you know that your body is in the past and that it is exhibiting the three dimensional support of what you were in attitude, OWN IT. Then, in a moment, you can bring your body concurrent with now. In a moment.

When you know that what you are you have created, that what your body is responding to is the genetic heritage you picked and have added to by your own attitude throughout your years, you will heal your body and manifest, simply by truth, the feeling that will bring the body up to now.

The master masters toward the Christ. He masters ignorance to become the knowingness that slowly and surely everything fits. When it fits, all is in full bloom, and the body is lifted, for it is vibrating at the same rate as the consciousness.

The reason the Christ ascended is because his body was caught up with his spirit. He attuned his body to vibrate at the same moment his unique demand in emotion manifested.

In learning to manifest, learn the science that you are living this moment in three different time flows: the body is in the past; the social consciousness is in the now; and the unlimited consciousness is happening this next moment.

How do you put the past, present and future together? Through knowledge. Knowledge that allows you to wake up. It is the only way.

Until you can come together and bring the past, present and future into now, you are going to have to live with what enslaves you, what you hate, what you are bitter toward, what you don't like, what keeps you from becoming ONE.

Every moment you don't like something, you lose the grandness of you. Every moment you are subservient to something, you lose your power.

KNOW where your allegiance and your limitations are. It doesn't mean change them; it means know them.

"Power to manifest" is taking responsibility and putting yourself together. Once you do that you will LOVE what you are.

Look at your life as an adventure, that if you changed any one thing about it, you wouldn't even be here; that it all brought together what you are this moment, and you love it.

There shall come an hour when you have gained all of your power back, you sit in control of your destiny, and at any moment you can change anything.

When the hour comes to learn to manifest and to embrace there cannot be a shadow lingering anywhere in that which is called I AM.

Everything about you must be understood in a knowingness flow.

Perhaps you cannot write it down or say it, but it is a knowingness.

A knowingness.

What is "I AM" ?

What does that mean?

What is it that IS all that you are?

It is not the god of yourself that you master.

MAN ALREADY IS GOD.

It is not the greatness of yourself that you master, nor the terrible-ness of yourself.

You master your incapacity for obtaining worth. You master your dis-worth until you become worthy.

You change the attitude of slumber, of limitation that keeps you from seeing this for yourself: the "cannots" and the "I don't knows."

Everything a master speaks becomes his next moment of destiny.

You will never attain genius if you "can't," if you "will not," if you "don't know."

Every action, every word colors the mirror that you are.

Part of learning to manifest is learning all about yourself. Know how powerful you are. Hear yourself speak. Imagine all the things you say. You cannot have unlimited power that only works in one area and doesn't work in another.

It is not that you wear a long robe, it is not that you wear ash upon your forehead, it is not that you dangle with crystals. IT IS WHAT YOU ARE – what is behind your eyes – that is the power. And IT is manifesting your destiny tenfold, the more you recognize it; a thousandfold, the more you acknowledge it; a millionfold when you KNOW it.

You cannot force it. It comes naturally when you become unified in accepting and loving what you are. Then it is simple.

When you become unified, all your energy begins to shift, to open, to reactivate the great seals, and the brain is brought to life from its dream. Greater consciousness is conceived, genius is born and the body stops aging because you stop being a duality ("I can't" "I don't know" "It's too tough"), and you become alive.

Gather your power in the unification of soul, spirit, body and personality (altered ego), and you become a working master. As you visualize and see the clarity, the more in focus you become, and the natural attributes of that are the endowment of power, indeed, beholding God, unlocking the kingdom of heaven and life that is forever and ever and ever.

Contemplate a little child who is caught up in the mirth and the zeal of living, and through the absoluteness of innocence seizes the world in harmony!

Children from two until four are geniuses. They see dimensions you are clamoring to see. They talk to entities you think are not there. They can create an entire city on grass. This is alive for them!

Manifesting is like a child. You bring all of your parts together and everything changes from the limited self to the unlimited self, to the little child.

You get back to this by owning all of your experience from puberty to this hour. When you own that you have life, you will cease to grow old. Your body will catch up with you because you are no longer "I don't know, I cannot;" you are "I AM, I WILL, I KNOW, I KNOW ," and you forge into the future of that manifestation of knowledge.

You begin to grow again, all hormones are brought into balance, your glands are clarified and unified, the death hormone ceases, and you become new. Your skin changes, your body changes, and you are caught up in the attitude of the little child.

The secret of rejuvenation lies in the genius of the will of the god that made it that way. WHEN YOU ARE ONE WITH YOURSELF, YOU WILL BE IMMORTAL.

When you begin, you manifest within the possibility of what you can perceive.

How wonderful to broaden your power to manifest according to what you know, because when you do it, and the manifestation happens, you are in zest and glee, and that joy has just expanded your mind. The manifestation is a testament that you have done it yourself.

What does that do? It allows room for greater thought. The mind comes awake. You come into focus. The next manifestation will be greater, and it builds and builds and builds.

To become a Christ is to become wild and free of all things because you ARE all things. You get there, not through the enslavement of another, but by polishing yourself. It is you who must make you happy. When you understand what you are and begin to manifest from that center, you are glorified. That is freedom.

I KNOW

I CAN

Change your destiny in a moment.

When you step out and take control there are many wondrous entities who come into your life. They are there because they desire to be there and your manifestation was the clay that made the castle to which they are coming.

Here you are, desiring your great manifestation and learning how to do it, and far, far away from here another entity has just had a fantasy, and in that fantasy lies what you are endeavoring to manifest. Since God's mind is the flow of eternity, and everything is in the flow, that fantasy will cross paths with your manifestation.

You are manifesting it for yourself, but it provides a door for some-one who is having a fantasy about it. That is how it works, for everything is in the flow, and in the mind of God, it is all moving forward. It is called eternity.

Manifesting perfection is a limitation.

Everything in nature is evolving. It is never perfect, and it has never been imperfect. It is in a state of evolution called forever, God Intelligence.

Perfection is a limitation because it means the ceasing of evolution. Nature evolves, adjusting continuously.

If you are learning to manifest because it is going to be good for you, or going to make you glitter and shine, that is a limitation.

"I DESIRE TO KNOW," moves forward.

Whatever you do, whatever you want, in having it, build your self worth to the majesty of a Christ, for there will come an hour that you will become so alive, so focused, so awakened walking in light, that in a moment, through desire, you can change the vibratory frequency of your entire cellular mass and leave this third dimension and go into the next.

When you awaken, all you have to do is see yourself greater, in a moment, and your body will begin to go back, reverse from mass into the lower electrum of light and the ideal of what you are manifests and in a moment you are gone. Ascension.

When you start with "I want, I desire, I am," and it is embraced and so manifested, you are taking the first step to Christhood, ascension. Everything works in harmony.

And when you become greater, when you see from above all that you are, you are going to do wonderful things.

Own that you are worthy of being God. Feel it, and do not quiver that you have said something wrong.

Take control of your life — desire to do so. Become God, the whole and the culmination of all life force — all that you are.

God is You.

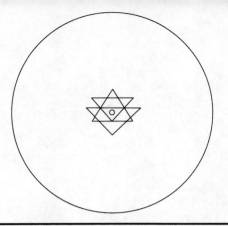

WHATEVER YOU MANIFEST YOU BECOME

Exercises in Manifesting

Make yourself comfortable. Lie, if you wish, or sit.

Look at your jewelry. If it is metal or stone, it carries the electrical frequency of emotion. In other words, it owns the past. It continuously feeds your auric field, thus feeding your consciousness. Whenever you manifest, do so naked of metal and stone. Take them off and put them in front of you.

Take your shoes off, because energy flows out of the body through the feet. Pain flows out of the body through the conduit of the feet, not back through the auric field. Take your shoes off.

If your belt is too tight, take it off. If your pants are too tight, loosen them. If you are wearing anything that is too tight, it will cut off the flow of energy in your body.

When you go to your place of solitude, to begin to enact this energy of manifestation into your life, wear loose clothing because it does not tether the body, nor does it cut off circulation.

Now you are going to "reason" the science of manifestation. You will learn how to go through the steps that take you into manifestation.

Your greatest manifestations will come when you are alone, when you are in a place that is peaceful and tranquil. Then this exercise will come into focus as a reality.

When you are in a room, it is hot, it is closed, it is a limitation. Nature is the wildest frontier to go into and learn to manifest.

What you are reading is an exercise. When you are <u>doing</u> this, close your eyes, become rested and comfortable, and begin to feel what you have read here. Allow your soul to call up the words and begin to visualize them.

This truth and this power are very simple. For eons it was consid-
ered a secret doctrine.

IN ORDER TO MANIFEST YOU MUST EMBRACE THE IDEAL OF THE
MANIFESTATION. EMBRACE IT EMOTIONALLY UNTIL THE EMOTION
BECOMES THE PHYSICAL BODY.

Almost every adult has had a sexual fantasy. Through the fantasy, you were able to recreate a scene so well that the body became alive and an erection was created as a result. That is how powerful a fantasy can be.

Anyone who has created a sexual fantasy, and in his mind has changed a partner, has brought forth seed and spilt it, has brought forth gratification to that point, all from the fantasy, knows the secret of the power to manifest.

So, contemplate a recent fantasy. Think about what you fantasized. It is not wrong. Just understand it. Go back and realize what the result of the fantasy was. Contemplate that.

The body is beautiful. There are many reasons you have had to create a fantasy in order to fulfill the body. What was the capstone of the manifestation? It was your ability to gratify yourself in passion, by a deliberate act of the mind.

That is how powerful you are.

God is not less than or better than.

God is the evenness of all there is.

TO MANIFEST IS TO DESIRE WHAT YOU WANT AND LIVE THE FANTASY
OF IT, EMBRACING IT EMOTIONALLY THROUGH THE SOUL SO THAT
YOU VIVIDLY BECOME THAT TRANSFIGURATION.

You will find yourself being caught up into another time. Your body vitals will change in the moment when you are caught and embracing emotionally and living the desire. You will know when it is finished. Your body will release the energy. You have elevated it to that same energy of spilling the seed or convulsing the womb, the same truth.

It takes the same degree of energy to manifest destiny's change, applied in a different understanding, that it takes to manifest the body into passion.

Go over, from the Lord God of Your Being, what it is you desire. Simply. What is the problem you wish to address? Then live the resolution in a fantasy, as intently as a sexual fantasy.

Do it now.

IF YOU WERE LOOKING FOR SOMETHING TO FOCUS ON

YOU ARE NOT READY TO MANIFEST.

Manifestation is the same thrust of energy that you have used all of your life, but without burning in the direction of a sexual fulfillment.

A powerful god can embrace the desire of anything he wishes with the same passion and the same thrust and the same desire as he does in the throes of physical fulfillment. It is the same thing. They both produce a reality. What your fantasy did before produced the reality for the moment. What you are desiring now and how you embrace it produces the same reality in a different direction.

Every entity who ever became, every master who became his Christhood, learned the simplicity of this power. THE SIMPLICITY OF THE GOD THAT YOU ARE. In order to learn this, you have to be ready and want to do it. If it flows from you and you understand it, you are with the flow. You will manifest. Wherever you are, whatever you look like, whatever ground you sit upon from the busiest marketplace to the highest peak of a mountain, you can change your destiny by doing this. It is within you at all times. If your dream is that you will die the following morning, embrace the dream and change it. You can recreate the following morning in the fantasy of vivid life. And so you change destiny. You have changed your past that is your present.

The Father is the simplicity of life. It is desire for perfection that creates the madness of intellectual comradery which denies one the practical senses of life.

Everything you have read here has been the breaking down of the complexity of unworthiness to gain a simple profound truth that unlocks the door to greatness, that every master who ever became learned.

This knowingness was lost because it was so SIMPLE.

Knowingness is not that which is written in unending verbage that means nothing. It is within. This explanation was SO simple, and that is why so few have ever found it. They never thought it was within them. They thought they had to go to secret schools, abstain from living, indeed, give themselves away in service so that, in the end, there would be a better life in the next one. They went to every measure except to enact the very lifeforce that is in an atom, to change in a moment, to become explosive into destiny.

Become the simple moment.

When Now is NOW nothing else exists for all past and future are merging in the moment. Yesterday is not yesterday, it is Now. Tomorrow is no longer conjecture, it is the reality of the moment, Now. YOU CEASE TIME. Where does "late" fit in with forever?

When time is stopped you grow, you open, the Father becomes and the greater you grow from this, the greater your light will become. Wherever you go, you can call forth in a moment from the Lord God of Your Being, and in that moment you can bring a manifestation into clarity.

In the beginning, you must get over the fact that it is simple. You must get over being unworthy or you can talk yourself out of this.

Desire to manifest becomes YOU so that whenever you open your mouth, so it is, whatever you feel, so it is.

Manifest taking the moment to have all time stand still to embrace your desire. It WILL happen.

When the master speaks a prayer, "Father, oh Father," he is invoking his original light, that which was his beginning, primeval light.

When you say "Father, oh God, unto that which I am, come forward," you push the buttons of the primeval light that you are, that comes from the soul into focus and awaits the command.

What you say, becomes. If you want the Source to talk to you, talk to It. If you want to know how powerful you are, ask you. When the word manifests, it pushes the button, the primeval cause comes forward and then allows and awaits the grand energy.

When you call on this force, that which is the Light, that which is the Power, when you call it forward with the command, it comes and the whole cycle of your body begins to change time flows.

You are going to bring into focus past, present and future that becomes the forever Now.

This is what the master says when he goes to his place to begin this dimensional fantasy embrace to learn to manifest:

BELOVED FATHER

BELOVED FATHER

THAT I AM, THAT I AM, THAT I AM,

COME FORTH, COME FORTH, COME FORTH

UNTO POWER, UNTO POWER, UNTO POWER.

I AM LIFTED, I AM LIFTED, I AM LIFTED.

BELOVED FATHER

UNTO THIS HOUR

UNTO THAT WHICH I BE

DO I CREATE

FOR THE GLORY OF GOD

TO THE FATHER WITHIN ME

TO THE DESTINY OF THE MOMENT.

SO IT IS.

Take the desire and embrace it by coming into the desire and living it until everything within you is caught up in the feeling, and time and space become a no thing — only the moment. Only the moment. And when the release comes it is "So Be It," for in that it is manifested.

When the release comes and the manifested is issued forth:

BELOVED FATHER

BELOVED FATHER

UNTO THE GLORY OF GOD

I AM   THAT I AM   THAT I AM.

SO BE IT.

IT IS DONE.

What is the miracle? I AM. That is the miracle, not "Maybe I am..."

I AM

SO BE IT

IT IS LAW.

The march of a thousand miles begins with a single step.

Find a place that is quiet, and sit upon the ground. The earth is alive, its electrical energy is vivid life. Remove all your bangles and begin to focus and ask yourself this question: Why am I not happy?

Say:

FATHER WITHIN COME FORWARD

POWER INTO KNOWINGNESS COME FORWARD

NOW.

Then ask yourself: "Why am I not happy?" and embrace what you feel like. From this comes the other side of unhappiness: a release into JOY.

SO BE IT.

When you allow the knowingness to push the button, then you never have to ask a question. You own all the answers.

BELOVED FATHER

UNTO THAT WHICH I AM

UNTO THE LORD GOD OF MY BEING

COME FORTH THIS HOUR

INTO POWER

INTO WISDOM

INTO KNOWINGNESS.

SET IT FORTH

FOR BE IT LAW.

SO BE IT.

ALL THINGS MANIFEST FOR GREATER PURPOSE TO TEACH US MORE

ABOUT OURSELVES, AND WHEN THEY ARE EMBRACED THAT WAY,

THEY ARE TURNED FROM AN ILL WIND INTO WISDOM.

There is a book called the Book of Life. It is the collective soul memory. It is what you have put together for eons of lifetimes. It is what you have locked up for so long and covered over with superstition, fear and intimidation. It is the original understanding of the great light which you are. There are no words for it. It is a primeval truth that you have gained but have forgotten. It transcends your alter ego of superstition, doubt, fear and unworthiness for the light is worthy of itself. It is called knowingness.

Sovereignty is the absolution of what you are. It is the same light of all grand intelligence that is in the mind of God.

If sovereignty comes to the surface, as you can command it so to do, it is your great pathfinder, it is your strength, it allows you to be lifted up beyond troubled water, and it will set you upon even ground. It is the light of God. It is the omnipresence. It is the foreverness of your character that is hidden like the bright sun behind clouds.

You can ask that your book open up and that there come flowing forward a feeling of divinity. It is as if you could reach out and touch the hem of God - it is that close. This flow is your heritage. This light, the light of Christ. It is that which continuously grows as one comes together from the limitation of past-present-future into the NOW.

This light responds to the spoken Lord God of Your Being. It quivers and comes forward. It permeates intellectual rhetoric. It permeates your doubt. It permeates your feeling of conspicuousness in taking a step outside the circle of the mundane. It has to go against a lot to come forward, but when you touch that essence of yourself through allowing it to come forward, without putting judgements upon it, if you allow the feeling to be there, it will LIFT you.

You are moving towards the epic of divinity. Your heritage was
never to war. Your heritage was never to scratch the meagerness
of survival.

YOUR HERITAGE IS TO BE GOD PROCLAIMED WITH DOMINION OVER
ALL UNDERSTANDING.

Unified Godman, Christ, the love of God, is not in the madness of following someone. It is the erection of the individual. It is the alignment of your divine purpose.

Above all your problems, your limitations, your wanting, your needs, your desire to be caressed, loved, touched, above all of that is the answer to individualism, to the self-sustaining of that which you are, the grooming of all the answers into manifestation and the freedom of self to exist in the flow of God, to go on to evolve into what you are individually: God in his most outrageous, most beautiful, most ongoing, forever form.

YOU.

The only essence that owns it all, that IS it all, is thought/light manifested in this consciousness. One who touches such light evolves to
an understanding that he is the all within the ALL that IS the breath
of every existence. Knowingness is the known of all known, but
here on earth, this light, your heritage, must go through your
dream: the dream of the disbeliever; the dream of the hard realist;
the dream of the lack of self-worth; the dreams of doubt, time, and
impatience.

When you are ready, there is no time. You will gather your great
light together, that primeval essence about yourself, and in the
sweetest moment you will bring past, present and future together.
That manifestation will be absolute because there is no longer
doubt.

"I am. I am," and it will be. No matter where you are, it will
happen.

God is not prejudiced. Your light is not prejudiced. It is without
judgement. It is forever. And it loves you.

"Want" is a holy word, for if it is sincere enough, it transcends all
limitations. Genius is born out of want. When you are clear about
what you want, there is no room for doubt. For those who are
ready, this is not hard, for desire born of itself is a need, and need
born of itself comes from want. It is an absolute alignment.

Come forth to embrace your prize like a warrior on a determined march. Embrace it, live it, feel it, become it. Go with emotion.

As you do, wherever you go you will find the power is greater and greater. It builds because the clouds that block your wonderful light become thinner and thinner and thinner until by manifestation you begin to live in a miraculous consciousness that is every day.

What you are learning is grandest in the early morn when it is quiet. It is potent before the hour of slumber and much is created. It is in the marketplace. It is in the valley. It is on the top of the mountain. It is at your labor. The more you become this outrageous embrace, the more powerful you become, the greater your environment and the more you become God.

It will be slow in the beginning because it will take you a while to learn how to embrace and to feel. The more you do it, the more quickly it becomes and THE MORE YOU KNOW.

There will come an hour when you look and it is. It is never questioned, it just is . And the desire is IS and it becomes. Then the master walks in the light of Christ. He IS. His word is law, and because he IS the omnipresence of all life, all life responds.

MAY THE LIGHT OF GOD THAT I AM

BE WITH ME THIS HOUR.

Breathe deeply, exhale deeply. Fill your lungs with light.

Find your own light, and once you are comfortable, close your
eyes. Only in the wildness of nature can you open your eyes and
still manifest. Close your eyes. It is important to look upon YOU.

What follows is the prayer a master speaks. Feel the WORD is
coming from WITHIN you. Look at what you are saying.

When it is finished, scan what it is you desire to embrace.

Desire what you want to manifest.

Then begin to live the future manifestation in depth, as though you
were an actor portraying a great part, as though you were manifesting a miracle. Experience the joy of that receivership.

See the unlimited. Live the unlimited.   Your body is filled with the
emotion of that moment, and you will know when it is finished for
the body's feeling will leave you like a wind.

If your mind wanders, let it wander. If you are focused, focus.
Live it.

When you are finished, when the feeling leaves and the vision
evaporates, so be it.

The prayer you speak:

FATHER

BELOVED FATHER

THAT WHICH IS WITHIN

THE LORD OF ALL

FATHER

FATHER

I AM

I AM LAW

I AM

I AM LIFE

COME FORTH

COME FORTH

THANK YOU.

SO BE IT.

When you are finished, say:

TO WHAT I HAVE DESIRED,

TO THE GLORY OF GOD THE FATHER WITHIN ME,

THAT INDEED IT STAND

WITNESS FOR ALL TIME TO THAT GREAT TRUTH,

SO MAY IT MANIFEST.

SO BE IT.

You limit the manifestation if you go back and analyze this, or walk back into it as the intellect and dissect it.

It is NOW forever.

When it flows from you, let it go like a river, for in the river, time and forever, so it begins to accumulate. YOU must go forward into the next embrace.

If you talk about what you felt, if you relive it, you have changed its destiny.

I AM is unquestionably I AM. That forthrightness in consciousness is ongoing. Nature never turns around and questions its life. It evolves. That creativity is the embracing and the harnessing of divine energy.

The moment of the birth of creativity into the cell of manifestation is the point when nothing else exists except the greatest point of pure emotion which you embraced.

It is finished. Like all life, it is the acknowledging of the existence, not the questioning of past existence. It is going forward, forever and ever and ever, as I AM.

Don't take it back and try to redo it.

Manifesting is alone, private, personal destiny.

If you go and ask someone his opinion of what you embraced, you lose it. You have given away your power. You have blatantly said that your worth is nothing because you need the credence of someone else to tell you it was terrific.

When you learn how to OWN this science, greater things than you ever dreamed of, no matter how far along you are in your life, will manifest and take you along turns, down roads of which you never dreamed. That is your heritage.

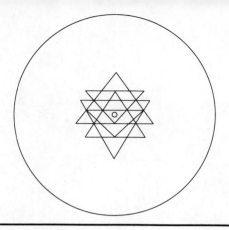

HOW THIS WORKS

HOW is this going to be finished?

The moment you let go of the manifestation, the light you called upon, the Primeval Father, Life, came into play. It IS the light. It is the momentum. It is the substance of all creation.

Mankind is the only species that has supreme dominion over all life and its awareness. This is a great truth. It is God Himself who has chosen this existence, and to have the knowingness of ALL his existences. That mind is the space of the atom's universe. It is all knowingness. It is the light that you have opened up. That light is the essence, the spark, the idealism, the momentum of creative expansion and evolution. The primeval essence called thought is in this light you have called forth.

What you live today goes out into the unseen, coagulates in light, manifests into a living organism and allows you the same fundamental linear expression you are enjoying now, except you have evolved.

Tomorrow cannot be captivated by science, yet it occurs, because life expresses its thoughts into emotion, and the emotion is the powerful electricum of light that lowers and manifests into the next moment.

You are the beating heart of God and every impulse creates time, tomorrow, distance, getting there, space in order to observe a reality from a reality.

What have you done? You have done what primeval life does every moment, except you understand how it works. That is the key.

The light that you focused on and embraced is set back on your throne in knowingness and governs the hypothesis of tomorrow with focused creativity.

When you are within the social structure you feed off of one another's thoughts. You are competitive. You are limited. The thoughts that set the premise for your next day are survival.

You do not include the premise of foreverness or immortality. You do not include cellular rejuvenation which can heal in a moment.

STRETCH IN KNOWINGNESS. EMBRACE THE WAY THE FIRST GODS EMBRACED — IN FEELING. EMOTION IS THE SUBSTANCE OF REALITY.

How does it work? You step out of the mundane into control and by doing so you create your desire. The beginning parts of its cellular manifestation, at this moment, are manifesting from the emotional light of that primeval being into a lowered reality of your desire.

You have stepped out of the ordinary, what fundamentally governs tomorrow, and you have changed tomorrow.

TO MANIFEST MEANS TO CHANGE.

It means you are evoking something different in your life. You have to go with the flow because you are the Lord who is walking through this creation, and you must walk through it ALLOWING.

ALLOWING. Allow it.

When it comes together, when tomorrow manifests through the imagery of your emotion today and starts to build what you want so you can go through it and deliver to yourself this emotion, this prize, expanded mind, when you can allow all those parts to come together, then you are a god on your way home.

THE REALITY YOU HAVE CREATED IS THE DREAM, NOT UNLIMITED LIFE.

Whatever it takes is worth it! If you can go through your manifestation and have the grace to allow it, it will stand as a testament to you. It is going to remind you that YOU DID IT.

And the moment you see it happen, you will begin to wake up from this dream because if that is possible, ANYthing is. You will stretch to know more, to embrace more, to become your heritage.

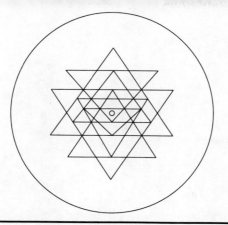

YOU ARE EVERYTHING THERE IS.

It is by your choice that you change.

Why are you learning how to do this?

When you begin to manifest, you will change your fortune drastically in many ways. To be rich is not necessarily what you need. You can only have so much gold. You can only buy so many things. When do you get tired of it? When do you lose identity with that? What are you are really after?

The gold, the things are there as touchstones in your manifestations. The manifestation is there to deliver back to you the same emotional impulse that you embraced through your touchstone. You could touch it. It was familiar. It enabled you to focus your three dimensional mind. The touchstone was there to make you feel a certain way. It, of itself, does not make you happy. It is HOW YOU FEEL ABOUT IT that makes you happy.

The prize of every manifestation is the richness of wisdom and joy that it gives you. It is not what is accounted for in the physical that is important. It is what occurs in the soul that you take on to forever.

If you desire a pot of gold at the end of the rainbow, you have to be able to put the pot in front of yourself and imagine what you would feel like touching it, throwing it into the sun and watching it glimmer, shooting off glowing rays that dance and twinkle in the light. You have to be that vivid. And it must make you happy to do that because it is through emotion that manifestation occurs. It will bring together the gold with that inner joy so that you may own it.

Your true richness is what you learn from it, and every emotion that you own becomes a pearl of wisdom in your soul. That wisdom stands as a tribute to you. You own that part of life, and there is more to come.

You can own it all by taking the step forward into change.

You can be as rich as you want to be. If your change takes you out of the marketplace and puts you on your own path, you can have all that you want. It is not a sin. It is not wrong to have money. Money is made up of the same essence as everything else. It is only your perception of it that makes the difference. You have to master the perception, own what it does for YOU. Then you will be free of it.

Or you can be as poor as you want to be. Or as mediocre. It is all life, and it is all even. It is what you need to prove your individual divinity that is important. That is why it is a game. Every moment you learn more about this game, the broader you become. And when you own it all, when you are too powerful to be enslaved, you ascend.

When you have lived all of life, all of the consciousness there is, you belong to eternity. And what is eternity?

Eternity is the all in all. It is the plane of a million mansions, meaning all in all that is forever and ever.

Anyone born of the flesh is endowed with the Christ spirit, and only until you are born of the flesh can you become it. That little game is the beginning of the master who masters all the things he needs, to own the emotion from them.

You begin to master instead of "I can't," I AM! Instead of "I don't know," I KNOW! SO BE IT!

You begin to change tomorrow and the uncertainty of time into how you want it to be, and when you own that rulership, you will unfold into the Christ which is everlasting, for if you can manifest tomorrow, can you not manifest the forever longevity of flesh? Indeed you do. The body goes with you. You end the life cycles because you no longer have to play the game.

When you embrace to manifest, you bring closer the quality of individualism that is divine. You bring home the song of God.

When hope and divinity and direction are restored, you walk out of violence into the identity that is clearly forever. You leave behind war - what would you argue with anyone about? When you embrace God you KNOW that everyone has his truth, that he has lived through that truth, and you understand and love him.

Love is not a word. Gentility and compassion are not simple gestures. They are the soul. They are the next step. They are LIFE! You have to walk into them to own them. And the closer you get to WHAT YOU ARE, the more you can look around and see the motley crew and say, "That which you are I love, regardless of what color your skin is, what your faith, what country you came from, what language you speak, how much gold you have or don't have." Strip it all away, and you have the physical evidence of a living breathing enigma that is part of evolution, a wondrous light.

Embrace that, for every hour you manifest and every hour you come unto the Father – " FATHER WITHIN ME" – you are calling forward the compassion, the gentility, the LOVE, that is the Father, that is life. You walk into that emotion, you embrace it.

What is it to be a light to the world?

It is to walk out of the dream into the reality of LOVE.

It is to walk out of the dream through manifestation, into the light.

The world is weary of philosophers. It is weary of ministers of a belligerent God. It is hungry to understand itself. It is ready to transcend from limited mind into unlimited mind.

To walk being a light is not a ministry, it is reality. Every moment of your life, and every step forward, every little manifestation you create, is a step out of violence and the mundaneness of the human trauma.

Every little manifestation, regardless of what it is, is going forward. The light broadens. It comes as a result of your daily manifestations. It is not by the word, but rather by the example lived, that you walk into the marketplace and find God in the beggar's eyes.

By that light the world begins to connect with hope. People hunger so for the spirit that they would embrace it because it is the hope they are looking for, and with that hope comes knowledge, and knowledge leads them from where they are.

You are hungry for what you are in relation to all that is, the truth of Self, your own individualism. Everybody is hungry for it. It is a hunger of the soul.

You will never prove a point by bickering over it. Who are you to debate another's conviction? It is greater to love him for what he knows. Allow him. That is compassion.

It is the individualism of God within you that allows you to be merciful. When you are, there is no longer the polarity of violence, and where there is a fearless entity, there is the awakening Christ.

NO ONE IS WORTH JUDGING.

NO ONE IS WORTH AN ARGUMENT.

NO POINT IS WORTH PROVING IF IT MEANS YOU HAVE LOST YOUR
STEP FORWARD.

If you follow, you will never learn to lead.

You will only learn to follow.

Learn the simplicity of how to change, how to interact with destiny and how to go back into control of the love of God that lingers in you.

Learn to love all people, to be a peacemaker, to see the world in harmony, to know the kingdom of heaven within you. When you walk forward you touch the gentility and the compassion and the hem of God, and what you feel, even in your darkest hour, will have the strength and mercy and grace to be in the continuum, and to let the love of God flow from you.

Go forward into the Father.

WHAT YOU SEE IN ANOTHER, SO ARE YOU.

If you are going to take control remember this: Whatever you perceive "out there" or "in here" - however you see it - so you are.

Instead of seeing the murk and mire within another, find yourself in
him. Look until you can see God in that person. No matter how
vile, how odious in spirit, how incredulous in society, no matter what
he has done, look until you find the beauty within him, the God, for
if you see anything other, then so are you.

Polish this wondrous self that you are.

If you can't see anything good about something, look for the purposeful good in it, because good and bad are the vacuum of one another and in the center is IS, and if you look at IS, you will find its purpose.

You will manifest when the fog is removed from the face of God that is within you that you can see more clearly, and the way you do that is to see the face of God in everything around you. Then it reflects back to you for whatsoever you see IT IS, it is the face of God and you have become.

Speak to the Father within you to find it in every moment, and when you do, you have made a great victory. You have come out of the dark ages. You are in Renaissance.

That goes for everything.

Everything.

When you come to such enigmatic beauty, you are the All, you see its purpose, you understand its dream, you know all about it, and there is no darkness, there is only love, there is only God.

No entity, no word, no intimidation is worth the loss of

forever.

Live for yourself. Become a light to any who want to look.

When things take on a harsh reality, remember that is how you want to see it. Mastery begins there.

Can you love your neighbor? If you are having difficulty, manifest the reason and own it. Don't judge it. Love it and bless it, understand it is all right. Love your neighbor. Embrace him. You think you have to defend yourself? If you do, then you don't own it. He is God. He has his right to an opinion. His whole life has been in judgement. He has been brought up in it. His government judges him. His religion judges him. It is a way of life. Know that and perhaps the light will come on for him that perhaps he doesn't need to do that, because YOU have abstained and through understanding you can still love him.

Nature is everything in synchronicity. The ecosystem of life is in a flow and a balance. When you walk forward, you walk into that flow. It is a flow of the whole universe changing that is the heart-beat and the pulse. It is a manifestation.

One who is in the flow, one who masters, one who becomes, who is manifesting, goes with an energy that is called forever, that moves, that is not perfect, it IS. That is the energy you are using. That is nature. And life. When you step forward you step into evolution.

Nature is not a threat to man. Man is his own threat. Nature and the earth are changing because of man's ignorance, his stupidity, and his NOT knowing. Nature is going to heal itself. Be in the flow of that.

When you walk out of the mundane, you leave fear behind and go into change.

Nature is the greatest cathedral. Have you ever had a tree judge you? Have you ever heard a great oak complain you are leaning on it?

The brook keeps babbling away, carrying upon it a wondrous, golden maple leaf and sitting upon this magic carpet is a delectable fly whose wings are burnished into an iridescent emerald as he drives himself down the river. Does it stop because you are sitting there looking at it? It is delightful! It continues!

Nature is the great teacher in silent slumber.

Want to learn what is in the wind? Want to learn the instinct of the fish and the wildfowl in their treks to places far far away? Go out into nature.

The water doesn't judge you. The oak doesn't judge you. The bug doesn't tell you to bug off. It allows you. ALLOWS you.

A tree doesn't know how to die. It would live forever. It doesn't know death. It reaches for the light.

If you find confusion in your life, go into a dappled forest, or a blazing desert, or under some great tree and call the wind to you. It will come and manifest knowingness without judgement because it allows you to step into its great domain. You will find your manifestations flourish there.

What do the great forest and the desert and the river all have in common? They are ageless. They are evolving on and on and on, and they have never said, "I don't like you, I don't like the way you look, smell, dress."

They allow you.

Nature, that powerful, everlasting consciousness is on the move. When you walk out in it, best be humbled by it. It is a teacher to you.

Be like every master who ever became. Find your conviction in the wilderness. Find a tree that allows you to manifest underneath and allows you to teach YOU in the quietness of its understanding.

TO LIFE

TO THE EARTH

FOREVER AND EVER AND EVER

SO BE IT.

There will be moments when you will question your sanity, because you will find yourself vastly different than what you used to be. You know more.

Every genius who ever crystallized an idea into manifestation was laughed at.

There is a breaking point to challenging the mundane. That is when you say, " HELP ME." The wind will come to you and be a mirror and a great truth for you to go forward in your own revelation.

EMBRACE THE WORLD BECAUSE YOU WANT TO.

Genius offers its own identity.

The idealism of Buddha Amin, Ra Ta Bin, Yeshua ben Joseph, Mohammed, the idealism of the Ram, the idealism of I AM seem like only a handful, but it is real. It is a tough road but it exists. It is an option.

There is help for you for as far as you want to go, to as much as you can obtain in every way you attain it, because a step forward is going back to God, a step to eternity.

The hunger of the spirit is not only to become self-sufficient through manifestation, for that is certain, but it also means that you take responsibility and broaden your knowingness, your wisdom, into genius. And that is remarkable.

Take what you have and cultivate it until it is powerful. It is simple to do. Manifest your kingdom, your joy, and if you don't under- stand something, ask it to reveal itself to you and it will.

This is all encompassing. Use it. And when the manifestations occur and they stand there, alas, as a great testament to you, give thanks to the Father within you, God the Father, for this manifesta- tion, for then you will be giving thanks and credence to YOU.

You are a blessing to life.

You are greatly loved.

You are going to do great things. Remember who is responsible:

The Father and I are one.

Remember I AM.

Remember.

So be it.

FROM THE LORD GOD OF MY BEING

UNTO THE FATHER WITHIN,

UNTO FOREVER THIS HOUR

I AM   I AM   I AM,

FOR FATHER

UNTO THE KNOWLEDGE THAT LIVES,

UNTO THE MANIFESTATION,

IT IS DONE FOR THE GLORY OF GOD,

THE FATHER THAT IS WITHIN.

SO BE IT.

GOD

I AM

FOREVER

AND EVER

SO BE IT.